SNOWMOBILE SNOCROSS

Darice Bailer

Lerner Publications Company • Minneapolis

Lerner Publications Company
A division of Lerner Publishing Group, Inc.
241 First Avenue North
Minneapolis, MN 55401 U.S.A.

Website address: www.lernerbooks.com

Content Consultant: Stephen W. Clark, snowmobile photographer and writer

With special thanks to Mandi Hibbert for her help with the manuscript and to racers Ross Martin, Mike Schultz, and Jennifer Pare for sharing their experiences. Thank you also to Marcel Fontaine, Trace Leighton, and Scott Erlandson for their knowledge about snowmobiles.

Library of Congress Cataloging-in-Publication Data

Bailer, Darice.
    Snowmobile snocross / by Darice Bailer.
        pages   cm. — (Extreme winter sports zone)
    Includes index.
    ISBN 978-1-4677-0758-9 (lib. bdg. : alk. paper)
    ISBN 978-1-4677-1736-6 (eBook)
    1. Snocross—Juvenile literature. 2. Snowmobile racing—Juvenile literature. I. Title.
    GV856.85.B35 2014
    796.94—dc23   2012049698

Manufactured in the United States of America
1 – PP – 7/15/13

The images in this book are used with the permission of: © Nathan Bilow/AP Images, 5; © Tony Donaldson/Icon SMI, 6, 23, 28 (bottom), 29 (top); © Stanley Hu/Icon SMI, 7, 22–23; © Doug Pensinger/Getty Images, 8, 9; © Underwood Archives/Getty Images, 10; © Robert Laberge/AFP/Getty Images, 11; © Carl Iwasaki/Time Life Pictures/Getty Images, 12; © Clint Wood/Brainerd Daily Dispatch/AP Images, 13; © Gary Walton/Action Graphics, Inc., 14, 24, 29 (bottom); © Jim Cole/AP Images, 15; © Paul M. Walsh/The Country Today/AP Images, 16; © David Zalubowski/AP Images, 17, 28 (top); © Jack Dempsey/AP Images, 18; © Sara Schultz, 19; © Steve Kohls/Brainerd Daily Dispatch/AP Images, 20; © Sean Donohue Photo/Shutterstock Images, 21; © Mark Bonham/Shutterstock Images, 25; © PRNewsFoto/Mystik Lubricants/AP Images, 26; © Steve Mason/Thinkstock, 27.

Front cover: © Moori/Dreamstime.com; backgrounds: © kcv/Shutterstock.com.

Main body text set in Folio Std Light 11/17.
Typeface provided by Adobe Systems.

TABLE OF CONTENTS

CHAPTER ONE

CATCH THEM IF YOU CAN

It was January 30, 2011. Snowmobile snocross pros Ross Martin and Tucker Hibbert lined up with the other snowmobile racers on Buttermilk Mountain in Aspen, Colorado. They were waiting for the Winter X Games snowmobile snocross championship race to begin.

As soon as the official snapped a green flag, the racers would be off. They would race 15 times around the 0.8-mile (1.3-kilometer) track. The track was littered with jumps, moguls (bumps), and sharp turns. The racers would fly off the top of one snowy jump and land on another. Snocross racers can soar as high as 30 feet (9 meters). That's about as tall as a three-story building. Riders can sail 100 feet (30 m) through the air before landing. The first racer to cross the finish line walks away with a gold medal. But snocross racers have to be careful. A crash would cost them the win. But that isn't all. A hard fall for a snocross racer could also mean a serious injury or death.

Tucker Hibbert
is one of the
best snocross
riders in
the world.

Still, pros such as Martin and Hibbert love the competition. They want to be the fastest racers around. Martin had won a silver and a bronze medal at past Winter X Games. But Hibbert was the champion. He had taken the Winter X Games gold medal in snowmobile snocross each of the last four years. Martin hoped to win his first gold medal that afternoon. Hibbert hoped to win his fifth.

Would Martin or Hibbert be able to beat the rest of the field to the finish line? The green flag snapped. But Martin made a mistake. He started a moment too soon. Still, Martin roared off with Hibbert and the others.

Ross Martin won the bronze medal at the 2006 Winter X Games.

Snowmobiles often run into one another in the tight corners of the snocross course, so racers try to be the first snowmobile around the corner.

Because of his early start, Martin had taken the holeshot. This meant he was the first racer to the first turn. This was a big advantage. Snowmobiles often get tangled up with one another at tight corners. Martin's lead would give him a clear ride around the first bend. Martin led going up the first hill. But Hibbert caught up to him. They were airborne coming off the hill. Now the pair was side by side, hurtling through the frosty sky.

Hibbert and Martin stood on their snowmobiles and bent their knees. This would help cushion their landings. Their sleds hit the cold, white ground. A flurry of snow flew up around them.

THE WINTER X GAMES

ESPN holds the Winter X Games, an extreme sports competition, every year. Athletes compete for gold, silver, and bronze medals as well as prize money. The Winter X Games are the largest action sports competition in the United States. The games are broadcast around the world. Pros such as Martin and Hibbert train all year for this event.

SNOCROSS FLAGS

At a snocross race, officials stand along the snowy track holding flags. Each flag color has a different meaning for the racers:

Green: Go! The race has begun.

Yellow: Slow down. No passing or jumping. There may be an accident ahead.

Red: Stop! Someone may be injured on the track.

Black: Penalty or disqualification

Blue: Lapped! Other racers are ahead and lapping.

White: Racers are on their last lap.

Checkered: We have a winner! Someone has crossed the finish line. The race is over when each rider has passed the checkered flag.

Robbie Malinoski soars past the checkered flag at the 2006 Winter X Games.

A black flag ordered Martin to stop at the end of the first lap. Because of his early start, Martin had to let the other racers pass him. Then he could jump back in the race. Hibbert roared off on his Arctic Cat snowmobile. Now the four-time champion could take the lead.

8

Soon Martin was able to reenter the race. But he had gone from first place to last place. A win looked hopeless. But Martin didn't give up. He gripped his handlebars and revved the snowmobile. He passed one racer in the group ahead, and then another. Before long, Martin had passed everyone but Hibbert.

An official waved a black-and-white checkered flag. That meant there was a winner. It was Hibbert. He had won his fifth straight gold medal. At the time, only one other Winter X Games athlete had won five gold medals in a row. Hibbert had tied the record set by snowboarder Nate Holland in 2010. Hibbert was the snocross king.

But Martin didn't go home empty-handed. He had come all the way back from last place to take the silver medal.

9

CHAPTER TWO

SNOCROSS HISTORY

Snowmobile snocross is a somewhat new sport. But snowmobiles have been around for a lot longer. They aren't used just for fun, however. In the early 1900s, snowmobiles were an important part of winter travel.

In 1927 Carl J. Eliason built a motorized sled in his Wisconsin garage. Eliason called his invention the Eliason Motor Toboggan. Eliason sold his toboggans to doctors, hunters, and forest and utility workers. But these motor toboggans still weren't very common.

Carl J. Eliason invented and built an early version of the snowmobile in Wisconsin.

Joseph-Armand Bombardier's early snowmobiles looked very different from modern snowmobiles. This one, displayed at a winter carnival, could carry as many as 12 passengers.

Bombardier's Invention

Inventor Joseph-Armand Bombardier lived in a small farming village in Canada. In the winter of 1934, his two-year-old son was very sick. The nearest hospital was 30 miles (48 km) away. Most of the local roads were unpaved and unplowed. They were buried in deep snow.

Bombardier needed a vehicle that was powerful enough to drive across snow all the way to the hospital. As a teenager he had created a motorized sleigh. But he had never perfected the design. With no way to get to town, his little boy died from the illness.

Bombardier was very sad. He was determined to perfect his snow vehicle. He knew that having one was a matter of life and death in the Canadian winter. Bombardier got to work. He created a snowmobile that looked a bit like a car. It had skis in front and two rubber wheels in back. It could hold seven passengers. And it could carry patients to doctors or cart children to school.

Ski-Doos were smaller than Bombardier's earlier sleds. People bought Ski-Doos to use for fun.

In 1942 Bombardier started his own company called L'Auto-Neige Bombardier Limitée, which became Bombardier Limited. He began making snowmobiles to sell. Country doctors, veterinarians, and ambulance drivers were some of his first customers for the new vehicles. Soon Bombardier made his machines big enough to hold 12 passengers. During World War II (1939–1945), Bombardier's snowmobiles carried soldiers fighting in Europe.

Snowmobiling for Fun

After the war ended, Bombardier began thinking about selling machines that could be used for fun. In 1959 he designed a new kind of motorized sled. It was smaller, lighter, and cheaper than his earlier machines. Families could use the sled for winter entertainment. Bombardier called his creation a Ski-Dog. But a printer made a mistake and called it a Ski-Doo. The name stuck.

Bombardier sold many Ski-Doos. In December 1961, Bombardier's company organized a fun race between Ski-Doos on a frozen river in Montreal, Canada. A new sport was born.

Snocross Takes Off

In 1979 the United States Snowmobile Association held its first snocross race. The racetrack was set up in Yellowstone National Park. It featured a winding course with a jump. By 1984 there were many snocross races throughout the United States, Canada, and Europe.

In 1998 the Winter X Games held its first snowmobile snocross race. Millions of people around the world began to learn about this exciting new sport. Many fans were hooked.

Two racers fly across the finish line at a 1997 snowmobile race in Brainerd, Minnesota.

CHAPTER THREE

SLED-HEAD COMPETITIONS

Canadian Jennifer Pare is a professional snocross racer. That means she is very busy during the snocross-racing season from November until April. Races usually take place on weekends. Every race has a new track for riders to get used to. Some riders do as many as 80 to 100 practice laps to get to know a new track.

Snocross is an expensive sport. Most professional racers ride as part of large snocross teams.

Snocross racer Jennifer Pare rides for the team Leighton Motorsports.

HOW FAST IS SNOCROSS?

At full speed, pros' sleds can fly down a flat track at 120 miles (193 km) per hour. But since snocross courses are usually bumpy, most pros go much slower. Snocross racers usually clock 30 to 60 miles (48 to 96 km) per hour. The jumps on the track slow them down.

Snocross races are divided into different classes based on the type of sled and the age of the racer.

Pare is lucky enough to ride on a team. Pare's team, Leighton Motorsports, has many sponsors. Sponsors help cover her equipment and travel costs so she can keep competing. In exchange, pros' sleds and equipment feature their sponsors' colors and logos. Some pros, including Pare, also have other jobs during the week.

Racing

The International Series of Champions (ISOC) organizes different competitive divisions for the top snocross racers. These divisions are called classes. Because few women compete in snocross, the ISOC combines the pros and the amateurs in one race called Pro AM Women. Pare competes in the Pro AM Women class. But she also competes against men in the Sport class. In this class, racers use stock sleds, or snowmobiles without any improvements made to them.

The ISOC hosts a race in November in Duluth, Minnesota, each year.

Each year the ISOC holds the AMSOIL Championship Snocross Series (ACS). The ACS is a series of eight races for the best professional and amateur racers in each class. The first race takes place in Duluth, Minnesota. The final race is held in Lake Geneva, Wisconsin.

In the ACS series, drivers compete for gold, silver, and bronze medals. They also earn points at each race. At the end of the series, the racers with the most points in each division are the series champions. Snocross has become so popular that fans can now watch the ACS on television.

Snocross competitions don't take place only in North America. The sport is popular all over the world. The Fédération Internationale de Motocyclisme (FIM) organizes snocross competitions across Europe. They feature athletes from around the world. In 2010 Tucker Hibbert became the first American to win the FIM Snowcross World Championship, held in Sweden. Hibbert won again in Russia in 2012.

Hibbert won gold again at the 2010 Winter X Games.

The Winter X Games

The biggest competition for most snocross fans and racers takes place at the Winter X Games. The fastest racers are invited. The snowmobile world was shocked when ESPN canceled the snowmobile snocross event at the 2012 Winter X Games. But snocross fans wouldn't be disappointed for long. Snowmobile snocross returned for the 2013 Winter X Games. Tucker Hibbert proved he was still the champion. He won his seventh gold medal in the event.

The Winter X Games does not have a snowmobile snocross event for women. But ESPN does have competitions for pros with

Blair Morgan earned his fourth gold medal in snocross at the Winter X Games in 2005.

SUPERMAN MORGAN

Blair Morgan won the Winter X Games snowmobile snocross event five times between 2001 and 2006. When Morgan crossed the finish line, he would kick his heels over his seat or handlebars. People called him Superman, because he looked like he was flying. Morgan was also a seven-time Canadian national motocross champion. Racing motocross helps snocross pros stay in shape during the summer. In 2008 Morgan fell while racing motorcycles in Montreal. His injury left him paralyzed and ended his career.

MIKE SCHULTZ

Snowmobile snocross racer Mike Schultz's life changed forever in 2008. During a snocross race in Michigan, Schultz took a bad fall. He injured his left leg very badly. Doctors were forced to amputate the leg above the knee. But Schultz didn't give up. He designed and built a mechanical leg for himself. His career wasn't over. In 2010 Schultz won gold in the first adaptive snocross competition at the Winter X Games.

Mike Schultz races in adaptive snocross at the 2011 Winter X Games.

physical handicaps. These races are called adaptive events. In 2009 ESPN held its first adaptive motocross competition. Motocross is similar to snocross. But it's a summer sport where riders race around a dirt track on motorcycles. Finally, in 2010, an adaptive snocross competition was added to the Winter X Games. Mike Schultz won the event in 2010, 2011, and 2013.

CHAPTER FOUR

GEARING UP AND HITTING THE SNOW!

To become a snocross racer, riders first need to get comfortable riding a snowmobile. It is legal for kids to drive snowmobiles. But many states require kids to complete training courses before hitting the snow. Young people should always ride with an adult when they are learning. When driving a snowmobile, pros and amateurs alike need to wear clothing that keeps them warm and safe.

A high school senior soars through the air at a semi-pro race.

SNOCROSS FOR KIDS

Pros aren't the only ones competing in snocross. The ACS offers races for kids as young as four. As young riders improve, they can advance through different age classes. If racers are good enough, they can turn pro at the age of 16. Being a pro means racers can get paid to compete. Pros also get to drive more powerful snowmobiles. Pros have the chance to compete against the fastest snocross racers in the world.

GREAT SNOCROSS GEAR

HELMET

Snocross racers wear helmets that cover their heads. They also wear goggles to protect their eyes. If it's really cold outside, riders will add face masks inside their helmets to stay warm.

NECK BRACE

A neck brace protects a snocross racer's neck from serious injury.

LEG PROTECTION

Knees need protection from all the twisting and hard landings. Snocross racers wear knee braces to protect their knees and shins. Most snocross racers also wear padded shorts or pants.

BOOTS

Snocross racers wear sturdy boots with strong ankle support.

CHEST PROTECTOR

A chest protector shields a racer's shoulders, chest, and back. All snocross racers must wear racing vests during competitions. These provide additional protection for racers if they are run over by a snowmobile.

RACING BIB

Racers wear a bib on their backs with their number on it so they can be easily identified. The number is required on the front and back of their sleds too. Like the helmet, the bib must have some orange on it.

GLOVES

Snocross gloves usually have rubber grips on the palms. This helps racers hold on tight to their handlebars.

Dan Ebert wears gear to keep him safe during the snocross competition at the 2009 Winter X Games.

Snocross sleds must be strong to handle all the sharp turns and steep jumps along the course.

The Sleds

A snocross racer may have all the right gear. But no snowmobiler will get far without a sled! Snowmobile engines come in different sizes. The engines are measured in cubic centimeters (cc). The smaller the cc, the smaller the engine. Snowmobiles with smaller engines go more slowly. The bigger the engine, the faster it goes. Most young snocross racers drive a 120 cc snowmobile. Most pros compete in a 600 cc sled.

Snocross snowmobiles are also designed to keep racers safe while they are riding. A special cord called a tether connects the engine on/off switch to the driver's suit. If the driver falls off his sled during an accident, the engine shuts off. The snowmobile stops. That way the snowmobile can't speed out of control and hurt anyone. Snow flaps behind the sled keep flying snow, mud, or rocks from hurting other drivers. Skis below the snowmobile help the sled turn sharply on the snocross track. A system of springs called the suspension system helps the sled absorb shock and handle the bumps and jumps of the snocross course.

Suspension systems help snowmobiles absorb shock.

Snocross star Levi LaVallee uses a huge trailer to haul his snowmobiles and gear to races around the country.

GETTING AROUND

Snocross snowmobiles usually weigh about 450 pounds (204 kilograms). Most pros haul their snowmobiles on big trailers. These trailers look a little like moving vans. A small trailer can carry two or three sleds. A big trailer can carry 10 to 12 snowmobiles at one time. Top pros such as Ross Martin have huge semitrucks or race trailers. Some trailers have workshops, kitchens, and riders' lounges.

Pro snocross racers often make improvements to their snowmobiles. These changes help them handle the courses more quickly and safely. Professional racers in some classes are allowed to change their snowmobiles, such as adding steel studs to the rubber tracks under the vehicle. This helps snowmobiles grip the snow.

Racers may make improvements to the suspension system. Pros also improve their engines and add top secret special parts to the sled to make it faster. Before pros race, snowmobiles must be inspected to make sure they're safe to drive.

Snocross for Fun!

Becoming a pro snocross racer can be a long shot. But snowmobiles aren't just for racing. Snowmobiling is a fun family sport too. Approximately 2 million people in the United States and Canada own snowmobiles. And many people rent snowmobiles. Almost 3 million people ride on North American snowmobile trails each year. The trails cover 225,000 miles (362,000 km).

It can be a ton of fun to get out in the winter air. Find out if there are any snowmobile trails near you. Maybe you could become the next big snowmobile snocross star!

Snowmobiling is a great way to get outside and enjoy the beautiful winter scenery.

LEADERS OF THE PACK

TUCKER HIBBERT

Tucker Hibbert grew up snowmobiling near his hometown of Pelican Rapids, Minnesota. He is the son of legendary snocross champion Kirk Hibbert. When he was 15 years old, Tucker competed in snocross at the 2000 Winter X Games against someone very familiar—his dad. Tucker won the race. He also set a record for being the youngest champion at the Winter X Games. Tucker is a six-time ACS champion. He is also a seven-time gold medalist at the Winter X Games. He has won the FIM World Snowcross Championship twice.

LEVI LAVALLEE

When Levi LaVallee was in fourth grade in Minnesota, he wrote a report about what he wanted to be when he grew up. He wanted to be a snowmobile racer, just like Kirk Hibbert and other pros. LaVallee started competing in 1994 when he was just 12 years old. He went on to become one of the most popular snocross stars. He has won the ISOC Fan Favorite Award two times. In 2009 LaVallee became the only person in history to try a double backflip on a snowmobile. He fell off during the landing. But he still won the 2009 ISOC Racer of the Year Award.

ROSS MARTIN

When he was five years old, Ross Martin started riding dirt bikes and snowmobiles in a loop around his Wisconsin backyard. As a teenager, he got a part-time job fixing snowmobiles at a local shop. At 15 Martin entered his first race. Five years later, he won his first professional race in the ACS. It was his first of three ACS wins. In 2006 he won the bronze medal in snocross at the Winter X Games. He won silver medals in snocross at the 2010, 2011, and 2013 Winter X Games.

JENNIFER PARE

Canadian snocross star Jennifer Pare started riding young while growing up in Québec. When she was just five years old, she sneaked outside to ride one of her father's snowmobiles alongside her older brother, Francois. When it comes to professional women racers, Pare is hard to beat! In 2012 Pare won the ACS and the AMSOIL World Championship Snowmobile Derby. The two wins made her the national and world champ.

GLOSSARY

AMATEUR

someone who participates in an activity for fun without expectation of payment

HOLESHOT

describes when a racer is the first one through the first turn in a snowmobile snocross race

LAP

the full circle of a course

MOGUL

a snowy bump or small hill on a snocross course

PROFESSIONAL

someone who participates in an activity as a job for payment

SLEIGH

a snow vehicle, often pulled by horses, with runners to travel over snow and ice

SPONSOR

a company that helps support an athlete with money or parts

SUSPENSION

a system of springs and shock absorbers to handle the jolts along a bumpy track

TOBOGGAN

a long, wooden sled with a flat bottom that is curved up at one end

FOR MORE INFORMATION

Further Reading

Carpenter, Jake. *Snowmobile Best Trick*. Minneapolis: Lerner Publications Company, 2014.

McClellan, Ray. *Snocross*. Minneapolis: Bellwether Media, 2008.

Older, Jules. *Snowmobile: Bombardier's Dream Machine*. Watertown, MA: Charlesbridge, 2012.

Websites

AMSOIL Championship Snocross
http://www.isocracing.com

This website has the latest race news and ticket information. The site also features pictures and biographies of snocross racing stars.

International Snowmobile Manufacturers Association
http://www.gosnowmobiling.org

Learn loads of information here about snowmobile trails, clubs, safety classes, and clothing.

Snowmobile Hall of Fame and Museum
http://www.snowmobilehalloffame.com/index.html

This website tells the history of snowmobiling. The site is full of pictures and stories about legendary racers.

INDEX

About the Author

Darice Bailer has written many books for children. She won the Parents' Choice Gold Award for her first book, *Puffin's Homecoming*. She began her career as a sports reporter and is especially fond of writing about sports for kids. She lives in Connecticut with her husband.